John Himmelman

FROG in a BOG

ichi Charlesbridge

For Caleb, one cool little nephew
— J. H.

Special thanks to Susan-Marie Stedman
of the Office of Habitat Conservation,
National Marine Fisheries Service.

Published by Charlesbridge
85 Main Street
Watertown, MA 02472
(617) 926-0329
www.charlesbridge.com

Library of Congress Cataloging-in-Publication Data
Himmelman, John
   Frog in a bog / John Himmelman
      p. cm.
   Summary: Features animals, insects, and plants in a bog.
   ISBN-13: 978-1-57091-517-8; ISBN-10: 1-57091-517-2 (reinforced for library use)
   ISBN-13: 978-1-57091-518-5; ISBN-10: 1-57091-518-0 (softcover)
1. Bog animals—Juvenile literature. (1. Bog ecology. 2. Ecology.)
I. Title.
QL113.8.H56 2004
591.768—dc21   2003003737

Printed in Korea
(hc) 10 9 8 7 6 5 4 3 2
(sc) 10 9 8 7 6 5 4 3 2

Illustrations done in watercolor on Arches 140 watercolor paper
Display type and text type set in Caxton and Barcelona
Color separations by Sung In Printing, South Korea
Printed and bound by Sung In Printing, South Korea
Production supervision by Brian G. Walker
Designed by Diane M. Earley

A frog is in a bog.

The frog hops from a fern and lands
with a plop in the moss.

Two mosquitoes fly away.

One mosquito lands on a sundew. The sundew curls around it.
The mosquito will be a good meal.

The other mosquito lands on a horsetail.

A dragonfly perched on the horsetail does not see the mosquito. It is watching a butterfly.

The butterfly drinks nectar from a steeplebush flower.

A muskrat tramples the steeplebush flower.

A mole cricket scrambles out of the muskrat's way.

The muskrat swims into the middle of the bog.
Two startled ducks flap into the air.

A turtle pokes its head above the water.
A fly lands on its nose.

The fly finds a pitcher plant. It looks like food. But it is a trap—the fly is food for the pitcher plant!

A kingbird watches the fly from a leatherleaf branch.

A hawk spies the kingbird from a tamarack tree at the edge of the bog.

It swoops down to attack the kingbird.
The kingbird turns and chases the hawk.
A bird-watcher looks on.

The bird-watcher picks a cranberry.

It tastes bitter.
She throws the cranberry back into the bog.

The cranberry lands near a ground cricket.
The cricket jumps.

The frog sees the cricket and snatches it up.

The frog hops onto a fern.

These insects are in the story.

flesh fly

mosquito

calico pennant dragonfly

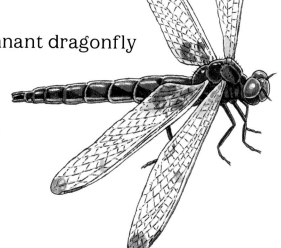

sphagnum ground cricket

bog copper butterfly

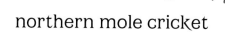
northern mole cricket

Can you find these insects, too?

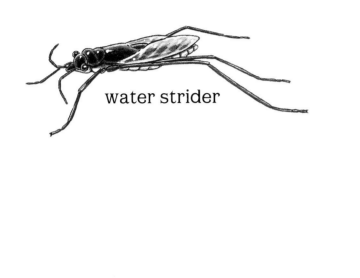

water strider

black-horned tree cricket

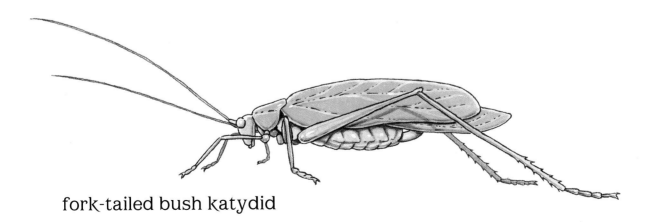

fork-tailed bush katydid

These amphibians and reptiles are in the story.

spring peeper

bog turtle

Can you find these amphibians and reptiles, too?

red-spotted newt

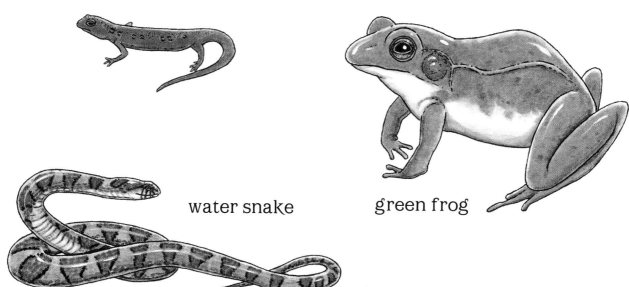

water snake

green frog

These birds are in the story.

eastern kingbird

red-shouldered hawk

wood duck

Can you find these birds, too?

red-winged blackbird

yellow warbler

northern waterthrush

These mammals are in the story.

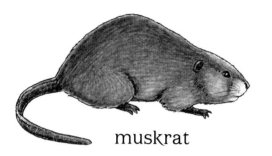

muskrat

human

These plants are in the story.

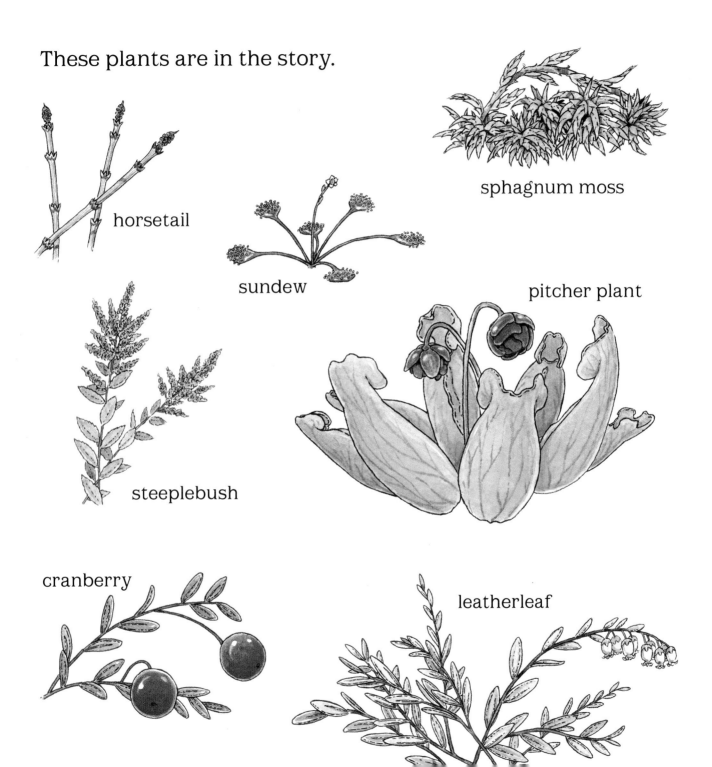

sphagnum moss

horsetail

sundew

pitcher plant

steeplebush

cranberry

leatherleaf

Can you find these plants, too?

horned bladderwort

grass pink

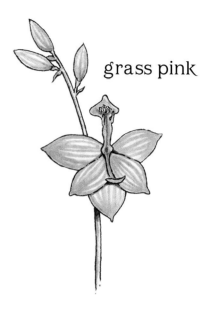

bog club moss

bulrush

sensitive fern

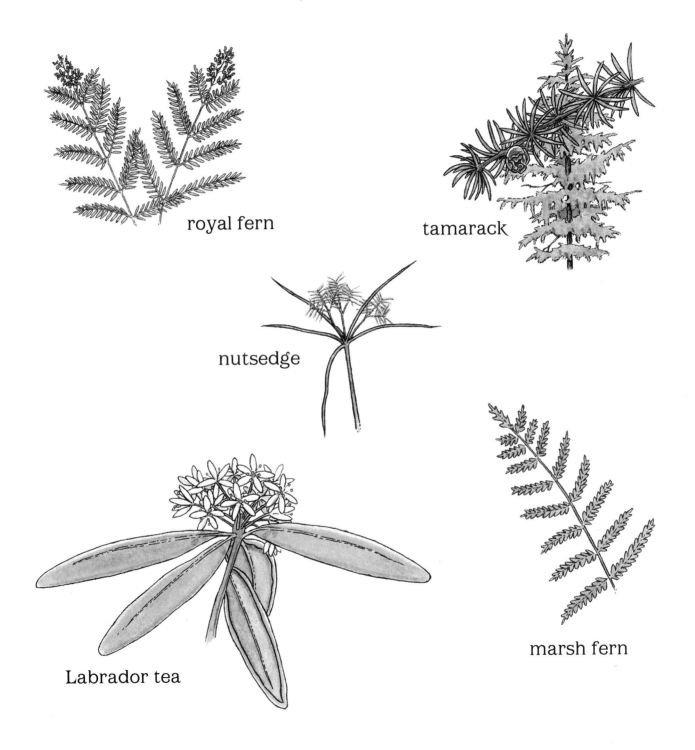

royal fern

tamarack

nutsedge

marsh fern

Labrador tea

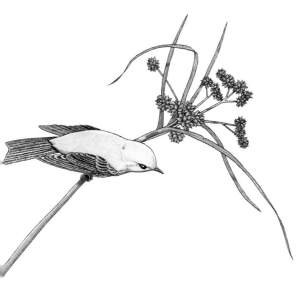

What is a bog? Most bogs were created thousands of years ago, when glaciers melted in low areas to form ponds. The water in these ponds does not get fed by a river or stream. Over time certain plants, such as sphagnum moss, began to grow in this stagnant, or standing, water. When the moss dies, it adds acids to the water. Most plants cannot live in places like this. The few plants that can have special ways to survive. Some can catch insects. Others can be dormant for years. This means they don't bloom and they don't need food. All of these plants, and the animals who live among them, make the bog a special place.

Visiting a bog is like visiting a different world. There could be a bog right in your own neighborhood.

Resources

For younger readers

Fowler, Allen. *Life in a Wetland*. New York: Children's Press, 1998.

Stille, Darlene R. *Wetlands*. New York: Children's Press, 1999.

For older readers

Eastman, John. *The Book of Swamp and Bog*. Mechanicsburg, PA: Stackpole Books, 1995.

Reid, George K. *Pond Life: A Guide to Common Plants and Animals of North American Ponds and Lakes*. New York: Golden Press, 1967.

On the Internet

Visit **www.eNature.com** for information on bogs and many of the species in this book.

The U.S. Environmental Protection Agency's site, **www.epa.gov/owow/wetlands/types/bog.html**, explains more about bogs and their status across the country.

Learn about all kinds of wetlands at the National Wildlife Federation's Web site, **www.nwf.org/wetlands**.